RE
D
OUT

IN ASSOCIATION WITH YAMAHA

CW01583719

RECORD DEALS OUTLOUD

IN ASSOCIATION WITH YAMAHA

The Music Industry Made Crystal Clear

smt

CHRIS BRADFORD

ILLUSTRATIONS BY PAT WEEDON

Head Honcho

Nick Raphael, Sony-BMG

A record label, contrary to popular opinion, is not a faceless organisation – it is a corporate structure that is run by human beings. Some of these human beings are those that commit to you as an artist and, with that, take responsibility for your career.

This relationship is essentially a 'marriage'. If either partner neglects their duty to one another, then there will be a 'divorce'. The 'pre-nuptial agreement' (or the record deal), therefore, is critical. It is the formal arrangement between you – the artist – and your record label.

Once you have signed such a deal, you will hopefully rarely have to refer to the terms of this contract – except to re-negotiate due to your phenomenal success!

My advice for having a successful career in this business is to get yourself a good music lawyer, find a professional and reliable manager, work on writing some great songs and, above all, enjoy your music!

Good luck!

Nick Raphael

Nick Raphael is the Senior Vice-President of A&R, Sony-BMG, responsible for signing artists from genres as diverse as Dance (Armand Van Helden), US Rap (Jay-Z), R'N'B (Lemar and Big Brovaz), Opera (G4) and Pop (Charlotte Church).

Disclaimer: This foreword is the personal opinion of Nick Raphael and not of his employer Sony-BMG.

MEET ZACK

"Zack's the name. Like you, I'm a musician on the road to fame, fortune and all things rock'n'roll. But it's not an easy road and many artists don't make the journey.

"So I am here to help you negotiate those tricky corners and sidestep the potholes that many musicians stumble into. Together we will uncover the secrets of the music industry and learn to avoid the most common mistakes made when signing a record deal.

"*OutLoud* is your speed-read to the key facts of record deals, so that you can spend more time writing and performing your own music and less time worrying about the business of music.

"In under 60 pages we will cover everything you need to know from what a record deal is and how to get one, to what makes a good deal and what makes a bad deal.

"Each page will answer an important question related to record deals. I will then explain each answer further and give you some advice as to what to do next.

"Armed with this knowledge, you should be able to sign the best record deal for you and your music.

"Then hopefully you will be on the road to fame, fortune and all things rock'n'roll - the red Ferrari, the celebrity partner, the sun-drenched villa in Spain and...

...the bumper bag of chocolate M&Ms (with the blue ones taken out, of course!)."

Zack

What Does A Record Company Do?

A record company discovers artists, makes recordings of their music and then sells them as compact discs or digital downloads to retailers and customers. In return, the record company pays the artist a percentage of each record sold – this is known as a 'royalty'.

Zack says...

"A record company helps you by giving you an 'advance' of money so that you can survive whilst recording your album. They will also pay for the recording, and the marketing and distribution of that album to the public."

Zack advises...

"Due to the vast amounts of money a major record company has to spend on recording and launching a new artist (between £100,000 and £1 million), the company will want a legal agreement with you to protect their investment and ensure they can make their money back."

Can't Buy Me Love...

What Is A Record Deal?

A record deal (or contract) is the legal agreement between you (the artist) and a record company. Its prime purpose is to give the record company the right to 'exploit' (i.e. use or sell) recordings of your music. It also states how long the deal lasts for, where they can sell your records, what costs they can charge you and how much money you will be paid. Most record deals are over 70 pages long!

Zack says...

"You can sign to a major or independent record company. Basically, the main differences between them are the amount of money available to promote you (more with a major, like Sony-BMG) and the level of artistic freedom you may have (more with an 'Indie'). Since an indie is privately owned, it can often be more flexible negotiating a deal than a major."

Zack advises...

"The crucial point regarding record deals is that they do not concern the songs themselves, but the *recordings* of the songs. It is vital that you sign a *separate* agreement with a publishing company for any songs you write."

Read this and sign please

So What's A Development Deal?

It is important that you understand what type of deal you are being offered. A typical record deal is called an 'Exclusive Recording Contract' and lasts for up to five or six albums. A 'Development Deal', however, is only for one or two singles and will give you little or no money apart from recording costs.

Zack says...

"A Development Deal is offered when a record company is not prepared to commit to recording a full album. Nonetheless, they may still demand enough tracks to complete an album if your single proves successful, and even retain the right to continue the agreement for future albums."

Zack advises...

"This type of deal is not so good for you. Whilst you are agreeing to a potentially long-term commitment, the record company is not required to continue beyond the singles stage. This is not as fair an arrangement as a standard record contract, so avoid having to commit to any albums beyond the first one."

Think of it as a development incentive...

How Do You Get A Record Deal?

You need to attract the interest of the A&R Manager (Artists & Repertoire). It is their job to find and sign artists to a record company. In order to get their attention, you will have to build a 'buzz' around your act by playing live gigs, recording a demo CD, getting press coverage and running an active website.

Zack says...

"The A&R Manager is one of the most important jobs in a record company. He or she is your 'hidden hero'. Apart from signing you, they will help develop your career, give you guidance on your music and promote you to the rest of the record company so that everyone works hard towards making you a success!"

Zack advises...

"Since so many other artists are seeking the attention of an A&R Manager, you will need to be thoroughly professional in your approach and ensure that any CD you give them is clearly recorded, looks good and features your best three songs. You only have one chance at making a first impression – be sure it's a good one."

Next!

Can You Record For Anyone Else?

No. A record deal gives the record company the 'exclusive' right to your performances as a recording artist in return for the investment they make in you. In other words, whilst signed to the record company, you cannot record for anyone else. In fact, *any* recordings you make within this deal period automatically belong to the company.

Zack says...

"You will usually be allowed to appear as guests on other artists' recordings but only if your record company receives a credit (eg 'appears courtesy of...') and sometimes a fee (known as an 'override' royalty)."

Zack advises...

"You will also be prevented from re-recording any tracks following the end of the deal for up to five years! It is essential, therefore, to insist that this ruling applies only to tracks *released*, not simply recorded during the deal. This will allow you to re-record any unreleased tracks at a future date in order to get a new record deal with a new company if need be."

...please leave a message after the bleep...
Great news, I've got the...
Record De....
...and that means you can only record for us now. Sorry!

How Long Are You Signed For?

Usually you are signed for one year, with four or five 'options' to continue the deal. The total perid is known as the 'Term'. Each 'option' period runs for 12 months, or until the release of that album. An album can take up to two years to come out, so a 6 album deal may end up lasting 12 years!

Zack says...

"When you hear about a band signing a 6 album deal, just remember the company is still only committed to releasing one album. It is the record company alone who decides whether to continue the record deal for another album or not – the artist does not have a choice in this."

Zack advises...

"Aim to sign for as few 'options' as possible so that you can renegotiate better terms at a later date. An indie record company will often agree to fewer options than a major record company. However, the contract still needs to last long enough to ensure the record company remains properly committed to you and can earn back the money it will have spent on you."

I said, we've agreed your Term...
I said, it's a never-ending Term...

What Countries Are You Signed For?

This is known as the 'Territory'. Most record companies expect to sign you for 'the world and the universe' – this is to cover satellite transmissions of your work! A small indie record company may sign you for just a few countries, e.g. the UK, or Europe, or the World but excluding North America.

Zack says...

"Signing an agreement for the World unfortunately does not guarantee release of your record in every country. The record company has to judge where you will be most popular and release you in those territories first."

Zack advises...

"The benefit of signing a deal for just one or two countries is that you can have separate record deals in different countries and choose foreign record companies that are genuinely interested in your music. The disadvantage is that it can be difficult to co-ordinate the release of your record by the different record companies in the various countries."

The Shetland Island
Tour 2005
Lerwick
Whalsay
Bressay
Scalloway
Yell
Foula
Fetlar
Unst

How Will You Get Paid?

You earn a 'royalty' for each record sold. This is usually a small percentage of the 'dealer price' (i.e. the price the shop buys your record for, not the price it sells for). You will also be paid a cash sum at the start of each 'option' period. This is called the 'advance'.

Zack says...

"A new artist or band signing to a UK record label usually receives between 15-20% of the dealer price. This is called the 'headline royalty rate'. If you are in a band, this royalty is split equally between all the members."

Zack advises...

"However, there can be many deductions made to this and what you actually receive is far less. These deductions will be outlined in your record deal. So, you need to find out what the 'real royalty rate' is *after* deductions, since this can sometimes work out to be *half* the headline rate!"

Keep the change, kid!
BUT Deductions Off HR include:
=Real RR 6%
or £48p

What Size Of Advance Can You Get?

The size of your 'advance' can vary greatly depending upon how 'hot' an act the record company thinks you are, how much they like your songs and whether recording costs are included or not. An advance of between £50,000 and £150,000 is not unreasonable for your first album, although it can reach four or five times this amount for highly successful or desirable artists.

Zack says...

"An advance is not free money. It is a *pre-payment* of the money you will earn from your record sales and has to be paid back using your future royalties. The good news is that if you do not sell enough records to pay it back, you do not have to return the original advance. It is the record company that takes the financial risks."

Zack advises...

"If the recording costs are included in your advance, be very sensible as to how you spend it, since you could end up not having enough money to live on – or even worse, not enough money to finish the record!"

Yeah, my CD sounds great but where the hell's the pizza you promised me?!

When Will You Be Paid?

Typically you are paid 50% of your advance on signing a deal and 50% on delivery of your recorded album. Royalties are only paid once you have 'recouped' – in other words, when you have re-paid all the money the record company has spent on you, including the advance.

Zack says...

"The record company initially pays for all recording costs, artwork, promotion, advertising, distribution and marketing expenditure, as well as any expenses you incur, such as hotels and travel to attend interviews."

Zack advises...

"Don't get carried away, though, each time the record company pays for you. Remember that eventually you pay for everything the company spends on you. The flash limos that are hired to take the stars to their aftershow parties are paid for by the artist even if the record company has ordered it. Taxi anyone?!"

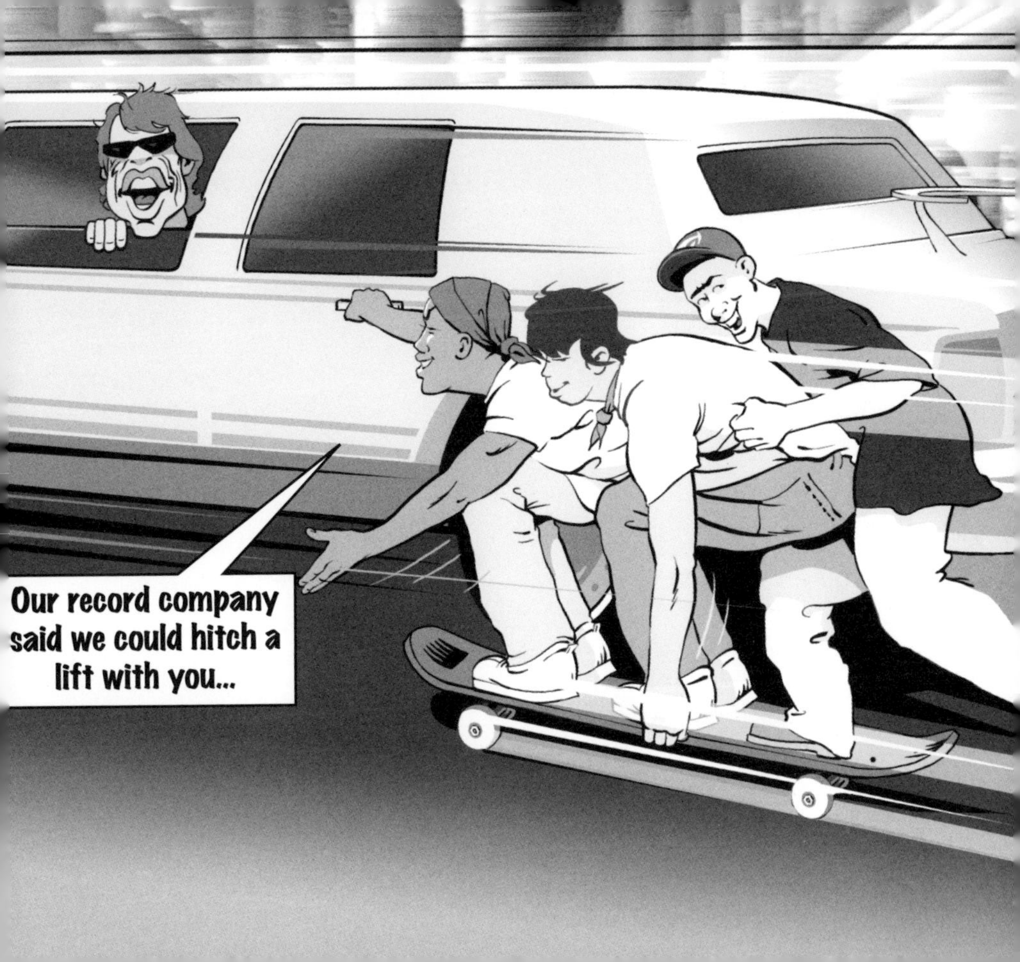
Our record company said we could hitch a lift with you...

What Do You Pay For?

In the end, you have to pay for everything. Costs from all your records are added together to form your 'record company account'. Any money that you earn from your records is used to pay off the total 'account'. This is known as 'cross-collateralisation'. In other words, if your first album failed to sell, but your second one is a huge success, then the money from this second album is used to pay back the costs of the first as well.

Zack says...

"There are a few costs that should *not* be charged to you. These include manufacturing, distribution, promotion and, for the most part, marketing costs (but not tour expenses, half of video costs and half of any money spent on TV advertising, which you have to pay for)."

Zack advises...

"The key point is not to allow your record company account to be paid off using money from any other source (e.g. tour or merchandise income) other than record sales."

Gimme the second piggy, that's mine too!

What Will The Record Company Expect From You?

A record company will require a minimum 'product commitment' from you in return for their investment. Depending on your deal, this will be five or six albums each with at least 10 tracks and a playing time of 40 mins or more. They will also want a certain number of extra tracks for use as 'B-sides'.

Zack says...

"The albums all have to be studio recordings (i.e. not Greatest Hits or Live albums), so, if your advance includes recording costs, you must think carefully about the number of tracks you have to record before agreeing to it."

Zack advises...

"The record company has the right to refuse your album if it fails to meet an agreed minimum standard. It is vital, therefore, that your contract defines this standard as 'technically acceptable' and not 'commercially acceptable' in the opinion of the record company. Otherwise, the company can reject your record purely because they do not consider it 'commercial' enough."

Sorry, can't hear the rapping
What rapping?!

What Does The Record Company Promise To Do?

After providing you with an advance and promise of royalties, the only other contractual requirement for a record company is a 'release commitment'. As long as your record is acceptable under the terms of your record deal, then the record company promises to release your album to the public.

Zack says...

"Release commitments apply only in the UK, since no record company can guarantee foreign territory releases as they have less control over these. Release commitments relate to albums, not singles, and will specify that the record must be released within nine months of delivery."

Zack advises...

"In a worst-case scenario, forcing a record company to release an album it doesn't want to is not going to benefit you much, since releasing an album without any serious marketing and promotional commitment is pointless. You therefore need to agree a minimum promotional spend in the deal so that there will be some guaranteed support for your album. This can be difficult to negotiate."

Released on the Isle of Wight!?
Coast to Coast

Who Owns The Record?

In the eyes of the law, because the record company has organised and funded the recordings and taken the financial risk, they are the owners, not you – even though you will eventually pay for all the costs.

Zack says...

"Unlike a mortgage on a house, which once paid back means you own the house, the record company owns the recording for 50 years (known as 'life of copyright') so that they can continue to make money from you after 'recouping' their costs. This is how a record company make their profits."

Zack advises...

"You will still be paid a royalty during this time, but you could make more money if you owned the recordings. The only way to do this is to record the album yourself and then 'license' it to a record company to market and sell for a set period (e.g. 10 years). The problem with this method is that you need a substantial amount of money to do the recording in the first place!"

If you want your very own copy, there's an HMV just around the corner

How Much Artistic Freedom Do You Get?

An artist's main concern when signing a record deal is usually the level of control they will have over their style of music, selection of songs, choice of producer, artwork and photos. A record company generally wants to retain as much influence over these factors as possible, so a record deal will state exactly how much control you have over any creative decisions.

Zack says...

"The four choices tend to be *a)* the record company has complete control, *b)* the record company has control as long as they consult with you, *c)* you and the company must both agree on any creative decisions, or d) you have complete control."

Zack advises...

"A new artist is unlikely to get complete control, but you should aim to agree to a mix of consultation and joint approval in key areas, such as choice of songs for the album."

This is my new direction - Lithuanian Nose Flute Jazz - I hope you like it

Who Pays For The Producer?

Like the artist, the producer is paid on the basis of a royalty for each record sold, plus an initial advance. These costs are considered part of the recording budget and therefore you will have to pay for them out of your own royalty earnings.

Zack says...

"A producer will usually get a royalty of between 2% and 4%. This is then subtracted from your headline royalty rate, meaning that if you had a royalty rate of 18%, and the producer negotiated a 4% royalty, then you will only receive 14% from the sale of each record."

Zack advises...

"In an ideal world, the record company would cover the cost of the producer, but this rarely happens, so try to limit your contribution to the producer's royalty to 2% and have anything above this paid by the record company."

2% - 4%
what's the
difference?
100%

What Is Tour Support?

Going on tour is very expensive and in the early stages of an artist's career, most tours will lose money. Consequently, a record company has to finance the extra costs of putting you on the road. This additional investment is called 'tour support'.

Zack says...

"Occasionally a record company may even 'buy you on' to the tour of a more established artist to raise your profile. This is a different, less acceptable form of tour support and one that is tolerated rather than encouraged."

Zack advises...

"Since a tour's purpose is to sell more records by playing the songs live, it is considered to be a 'promotional' expense. Unlike other marketing and promotional costs, however, which are paid by the record company, you have to pay back all tour support out of your royalties. So once again, be aware of how much you are spending. Room service or take-out – it's your wallet!"

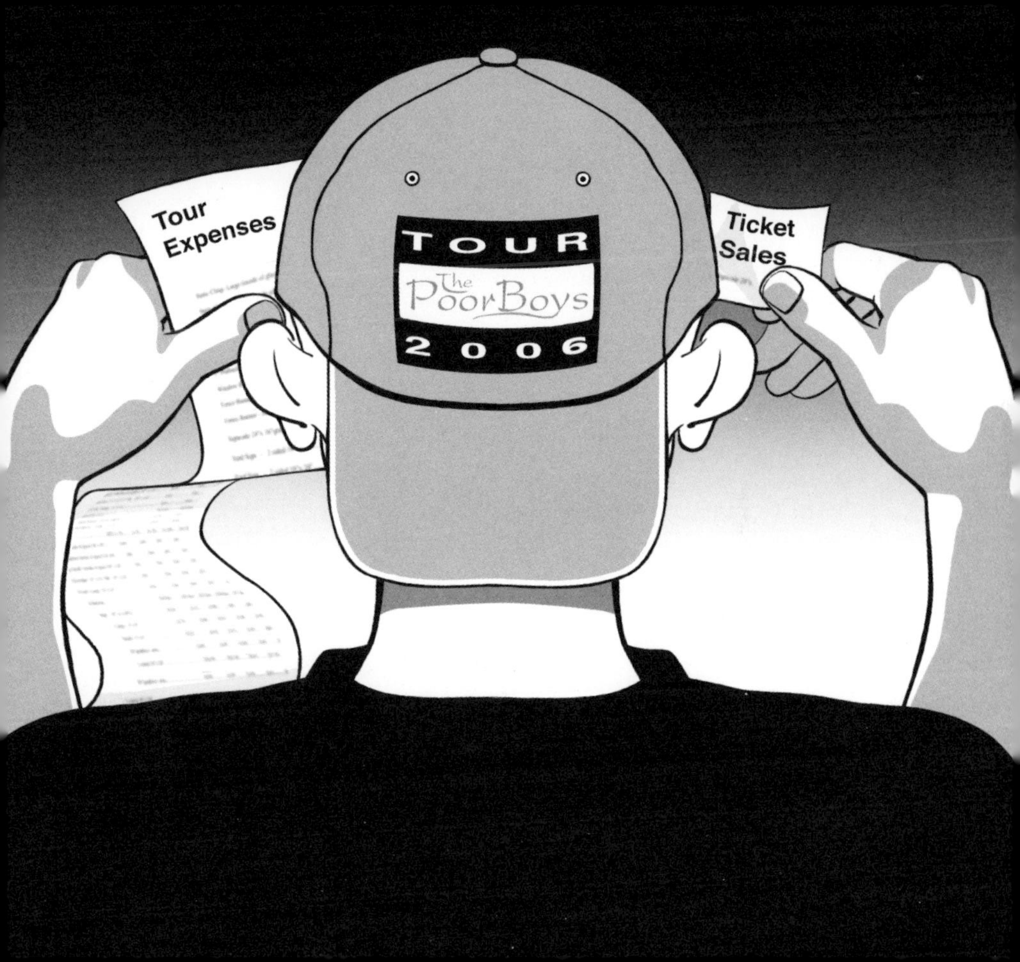
Tour
Expenses
TOUR
The
PoorBoys
2006
Ticket
Sales

What Happens If The Band Splits Up?

A record company signs a band both 'jointly and severally' – in other words, each member is individually signed to the record company as well as being signed as a band. If the group splits up, it is the record company who then decides which members it wants to keep under contract.

Zack says...

"The record company also controls any solo projects that you may do outside of the band."

Zack advises...

"If the record company does want to keep you as a solo artist, then ensure that the contract states you get the full royalty on any of these projects, and not the split share you would have got as a band."

The Russ Rodgers Band
We'll keep you, you and you, but not you, Russ!

Is There Another Way?

There is an alternative record deal that works on 'profit-sharing' rather than the standard royalty system. The record company still pays for everything and takes the financial risk, but this time you and the company split any profits made equally between you. With this type of deal you may receive an advance, but it tends to be smaller.

Zack says...

"In working out the 'profit' to be split, be aware that the record company deducts *all* costs related to your record including marketing, promotion, manufacturing and distribution. The standard royalty deal will exclude such costs and therefore you will not have to pay them."

Zack advises...

"If you are successful as an artist, then a profit-share deal can earn you much more than a standard royalty agreement. However, only an indie would be interested in offering such a deal. If you do choose this type of deal, then you must establish exactly what costs will be deducted."

One for you three for me
One for you one for me

Do You Even Need A Record Deal?

With the professional capabilities of home recording equipment and the promotional opportunities of the Internet, more and more artists are recording, releasing and distributing their own records without the help of an established record company.

Zack says...

"You will need a lot of time, energy and money to succeed this way, but you can make much more money in the early stages. With a basic record deal, you could earn up to £1 a record; with a 'profit share' deal this could get to £2 per record; but by doing it all yourself you could make £5 or more a record!"

Zack advises...

"Releasing your own record can be the best way to kick start your music career. If you do make a good album on your own and then a record label comes to you, you can negotiate a bigger advance, a higher royalty rate and still own the recording! What could be better!"

'GOING IT ALONE'
The DIY BAND
Now available from all friends of the band

Major Record Companies

Zack says...

"There are only four official major record companies, but they represent almost 80% of the music sold. Each of these majors is divided into a number of different record labels, such as EMI's Parlophone label. Each label represents a different genre of music. Visit their websites to discover which artists they represent."

The four major record companies are:

- Sony-BMG Music Entertainment Ltd — www.sonybmg.com
- EMI Music Ltd — www.emigroup.com
- Warner Music Group — www.wmg.com
- Universal Music Group — www.umusic.com

Independent Record Companies

Zack says...

"There are hundreds of fantastic independent labels to choose from. Here are just a few of them. Before sending your demo to one of these record companies, do remember to first check what type of music they represent. You can do this by checking out their website."

Some of the more established independent record companies include:

- Beggars Banquet www.beggars.com
- Domino www.dominorecordco.com
- Ninja Tunes www.ninjatune.net
- Rough Trade www.roughtraderecords.com
- Sanctuary Records www.sanctuarygroup.com
- V2 Records www.v2music.com

Useful Music Industry Organisations

Zack says...

"There are a number of music industry organisations that deal with record companies, and you may wish to contact them for further information. These are..."

- **BPI (British Phonographic Industry)** – the British record industry's trade association, representing thousands of British record companies, from the largest corporation down to the smallest label. Website: www.bpi.co.uk

- **AIM (Association Of Independent Music)** – a non-profit-making trade organisation representing independent record companies and distributors in the UK. Website: www.musicindie.org

- **MU (Musicians' Union)** – a trade association that has represented and protected UK musicians of all types for over 100 years. Website: www.musiciansunion.org.uk

Further Reading

Zack says...

"If, after reading this book, you wish to learn more about record deals and the music business, then I recommend the following books..."

- *How To Succeed In The Music Business* by Allan Dann & John Underwood (Omnibus Press)
- *The Band's Guide To Getting A Record Deal* by Will Ashurst (Sanctuary Publishing)
- *Heart & Soul: Revealing The Craft Of Songwriting* by Chris Bradford (Sanctuary Publishing)

Other books in the OutLoud series include:

- *Artist Management OutLoud* (SMT)
- *Music Publishing OutLoud* (SMT)

ACM
THE ACADEMY OF CONTEMPORARY MUSI
Full and Part time courses in: Guita
Bass, Drums , Vocal
Music Production, DJ Skills an
Music Busines
EAT.
SLEEP.
DRINK.
LEARN
THE RODBORO BUILDINGS BRIDGE STREET GUILDFORD SURREY UK GU14
01483 500 800 | ENQUIRIES@ACM.AC.UK | WWW.ACM.AC.U

For serious musicians, songwriters and producers the world over, Yamaha musical instruments and music technology have become synonymous with quality and creativity. Yamaha plays an important role in the creative and recording process and our development people pay close attention to the current and future needs of musicians everywhere.

We are proud of our supportive relationships with emerging and established talent, and hope that this exciting OUTLOUD series will assist all those seeking an audience to better navigate the nuances and complexities of the music business good luck!

Keep writing and keep playing - if you've got it they want it!

For more information on Yamaha instruments, equipment and music support schemes please visit www.yamaha-music.co.uk

YAMAHA

ESSENTIAL TOOLS

Published by **SMT**
an imprint of Bobcat Books Limited
8/9 Frith Street, London W1D 3JB, UK.

Exclusive Distributors:
Music Sales Limited
Distribution Centre, Newmarket Road, Bury St Edmunds, Suffolk IP33 3YB, UK.

Music Sales Corporation
257 Park Avenue South, New York, NY10010, USA.

Music Sales Pty Limited
120 Rothschild Avenue, Rosebery, NSW 2018, Australia.

Order No. SMT2233
ISBN 1-84609-530-1
This book © Copyright 2006 Bobcat Books Limited,
a division of Music Sales Limited.

All rights reserved. No part of this book may be reproduced in any form or by any electronic or mechanical means, including information storage or retrieval systems, without the permission in writing from the publisher, except by a reviewer, who may quote brief passages

Printed in the EU

Your Guarantee of Quality
As publishers, we strive to produce every book to the highest commercial standards. Throughout, the printing and binding have been planned to ensure a sturdy, attractive publication which should give years of enjoyment. If your copy fails to meet our high standards, please inform us and we will gladly replace it.

www.musicsales.com